chasing after butterflies…

going exploring…

standing on their hind legs
and listening to the wind
whistling in the meadow.

Bunnies love
tasting cool watercress
by a babbling brook.

Bunnies love
munching rhubarb,

crunching carrots,

nibbling cabbages

and alfalfa.

Bunnies love
playing hide-and-seek…

napping in a heap...

leaping over daffodils…

and sniffing at dandelions.

Bunnies love
dancing in the
moonlight.

Bunnies love
cuddling up to you
and having their soft
ears stroked
ever so gently—